A Book of Five Rings (Go Rin No Sho)

Written by Miyamoto Musashi

Contents

Introduction

It is now during the first ten days of the tenth month in the twentieth year of Kanei (1645). I am sixty years old and I have been training many years in the Way of strategy called Ni Ten Ichi Ryu. I will now explain it in writing for the first time. I have climbed mountain Iwato of Higo in Kyushu to pray to Kwannon and kneel before Buddha. I am a warrior of Harima province, Shinmen Musashi No Kami Fujiwara No Geshin.

Since I was a youth my heart has been drawn toward the Way of strategy. My first duel took place at age thirteen when I struck down a strategist of the Shinto school, one Arima Kihei. I was sixteen when I struck down an able strategist, Tadashima Akiyama, and when I was twenty-one I went up to the capital and met all manner of strategists, never once failing to win in many contests. After that I went from province to province, dueling with strategists of various schools, and not once did I fail to win though I had as many as sixty encounters.

When I reached age thirty I looked back on my past and realized the previous victories were not due to my having mastered strategy. Perhaps they resulted from natural ability, or the order of heaven, or in that other schools' strategy was inferior. After this I studied morning and evening searching for the principle, and came to realize the Way of strategy when I was fifty.

Since then I have lived without following any particular Way. Thus with the virtue of strategy I can now practice many arts and abilities without the need for a teacher. In writing this book I did not use the law of Buddha or the teachings of Confucius, neither old war chronicles nor books on martial tactics. My purpose in writing is to explain the true spirit of this Ichi School as it is mirrored in the Way of heaven and Kwannon.

The time is the night of the tenth day of the tenth month, at the hour of the tiger (3-5 a.m.)

Introduction

Introduction

The Ground Book

Strategy is the craft of the warrior. Commanders must enact the craft, and troopers should know this Way. There is no warrior in the world today that really understands the Way of strategy.

There are various Ways. There is the Way of salvation by the law of Buddha, the Way of Confucius governing the Way of learning, the Way of healing as a doctor, the Way of Waka teaching as a poet, as well as tea, archery, and many arts and skills. Every man should practice as he feels inclined.

It is said that the warrior's way is the twofold Way of pen and sword, and he should have a taste for both Ways. Even if a man has no natural ability, he can be a warrior by sticking assiduously to both divisions of the Way. Generally speaking, the Way of the warrior is to determinedly accept death. Although others (women, peasants and lowlier folk) have been known to die readily in the cause of duty or out of shame, the warrior is different. The warrior is different in that studying the Way of strategy is based on overcoming men. By winning in crossing swords with individuals, or enjoining battle with large numbers, the warrior attains power and fame for himself and for his lord. This is the virtue of strategy.

The Way of Strategy

In China and Japan practitioners of the Way have been known as "masters of strategy". Warriors must learn this Way.

Recently there have been people claiming to be strategists, but they are usually just sword-fencers. In olden times, strategy was listed among the Ten Abilities and Seven Arts as a beneficial practice. Strategy was certainly an art but as a beneficial practice it was not limited only to sword fencing. Indeed, the true value of sword fencing cannot be seen within the confines of sword-fencing technique.

If we look at the world we see that men use equipment to sell themselves. In this type of Way of strategy, they are looking for profit, and both those teaching and those learning the way are concerned with coloring and showing off their technique. Someone once said "Immature strategy is the cause of grief". That was a true saying.

There are four Ways in which men pass through life: as gentlemen, farmers, artisans and merchants.

First is the way of the farmer. Using agricultural instruments, he sees springs through to autumns with an eye on the changes of season.

Second is the Way of the merchant. The wine maker obtains his ingredients and puts them to use to make his living. The Way of the merchant is always to live by taking profit.

Third is the gentleman warrior, carrying the weaponry of his Way. The Way of the warrior is to master the virtue of his weapons. He must have a leaning toward strategy, for if a gentleman dislikes strategy he will not appreciate the benefit of weaponry.

Fourth is the Way of the artisan. The Way of the carpenter is to become proficient in the use of his tools, first to lay his plans with a true measure and then perform his work according to plan. Thus he passes through life.

These are the four Ways of the gentleman, the farmer, the artisan and the merchant.

Comparing the Way of the Carpenter to Strategy

The comparison with carpentry is through the connection with houses. The carpenter uses a master plan of the building, and the Way of strategy is similar in this manner of planning. If you want to learn the craft of war, study this book with a view of the teacher as a needle, the disciple as thread. You must practice constantly.

Like the foreman carpenter, the commander must know natural rules, and the rules of the country, and the rules of houses. This is the Way of the foreman.

The foreman carpenter must know the architectural theory of towers and temples, the plans of palaces, and must employ men to build houses. The Way of the foreman carpenter is the same as the Way of the commander of a warrior house.

In the construction of houses, one must choose the wood. Straight, unknotted timber of good appearance is used for revealed pillars; straight timber with small defects is used for the inner pillars. Timber of the finest appearance, even if a little weak, is used for the thresholds, lintels, doors, sliding doors, and so on. Good strong timber, though it be gnarled and knotted, can always be used discreetly in construction. Timber which is weak or knotted throughout should be used as scaffolding, and later for firewood.

The foreman carpenter allots his men work according to their ability. Floor layers, makers of sliding doors, thresholds and lintels, ceilings and so on. Those of poor ability lay the floor joist, and those of lesser ability carve wedges and do such miscellaneous work. If the foreman knows and deploys his men well, the finished work will be good.

The foreman should take into account the abilities and limitations of his men, circulating among them and asking nothing unreasonable. He should know their morale and spirit, and encourage them when necessary. This is the same as the principle of strategy.

The Way of Strategy

Like a trooper, the carpenter sharpens his own tools. He carries his equipment in his toolbox, and works under the direction of his foreman. He makes columns and girders with an axe, shapes floorboards and shelves with a plane, cuts fine openwork and carvings accurately, giving as excellent a finish as his skill will allow. This is the craft of carpenters. When the carpenter becomes skilled and understands measures, he can become a foreman. These are the specialties of the carpenter. Things are similar for the trooper. You ought to think deeply about this.

The attainment of the carpenter is that his work is not warped, that the joints are not misaligned, and that the work is truly planed so that it meets well and is not merely finished in sections. This is essential.

If you want to learn this Way, deeply consider the things written in this book one at a time. You must do sufficient research.

Outline of the Five Books of this Book of Strategy

The Way is shown in five books concerning different aspects. These books are Ground, Water, Fire, Tradition (Wind) and Void.

In the Ground book, the body of the Way of strategy is explained from the viewpoint of my Ichi School. The true Way is not realized through sword fencing alone. One must know the smallest things and the biggest things, the shallowest things and the deepest things. As if it were a straight road mapped out on the ground, the first book is called the Ground book.

Second is the Water book. With water as the basis, the spirit becomes like water. Water adopts the shape of its receptacle; sometimes it is a trickle, sometimes a wild sea. Water has a clear blue color, and through its clarity the truths of my Ichi School are revealed in this book.

If you master the principles of sword fencing, when you freely beat one man, you can beat any man in the world. The spirit of defeating a man is the same for ten million men. The accomplished strategist makes small things into big things; the principle of strategy is that knowing one thing is to know ten thousand things. I cannot write in detail how this is done.

Third is the Fire book. This book is about fighting. The spirit of fire is fierce whether the fire be small or big; and so it is with battles. The Way of battles is the same for fights between two men as for ten thousand to-a-side battles. You must appreciate that spirit can become big or small. What is big is easy to perceive; what is small is difficult to perceive. In short, it is difficult for large numbers of men to change position, so their movements can be easily predicted. An individual can easily change his mind, so his movements are difficult to predict. It is important to grasp this.

The core of this book is that you must train day and night in order to make quick decisions. Strategy entails treating training as a part of normal life with your spirit unchanging. Thus combat in battle is described in the Fire book.

Fourth is the Wind book. This book is not concerned with the Ichi School but with other schools of strategy. By Wind I mean old traditions, present-day traditions, and family traditions of strategy. Thus I clearly explain the strategies of the world. It is difficult to know yourself if you do not know others.

There are sidetracks to all Ways. If you study a Way daily, and your spirit diverges, you may think you are obeying a good way, but objectively it is not the true Way. If you are following the true Way and diverge a little, this will later become a large divergence.

Other strategies have come to be thought of as mere sword fencing, however the benefit of my strategy, although it includes sword fencing, lies in a separate principle. Thus I explain what is commonly meant by strategy in other schools in the Tradition (Wind) book.

Fifth is the book of the Void. By Void I mean that which has no beginning and no end. Attaining this principle means not attaining the principle. The Way of strategy is the Way of nature. When you appreciate the power of nature and are in tune with the rhythm of any situation, you will be able to hit the enemy naturally and strike naturally. All this is the Way of the Void. I intend to show how to follow the true Way according to nature in the book of the Void.

The Name Ichi Ryu Ni To (One school – Two swords)

Warriors, both commanders and troopers, carry two swords at their belt. In the olden days these were called the long sword and the sword; nowadays they are known as the sword and the companion sword. "Nito Ichi Ryu" shows the advantage of using both swords.

Students of the Ichi School Way of strategy should train from the start with the sword and long sword in either hand. This is the truth: when you sacrifice your life, you must make fullest use of your weaponry. Not to do so, and to die with a weapon not yet drawn, is false.

If you hold a sword with both hands, it is difficult to wield it freely to left and right, so my method is to carry the sword in one hand. This does not apply to large weapons such as the spear or halberd (weapons that are carried out of doors), but swords and companion swords can be carried in one hand. It is encumbering to hold a sword in both hands when you are on horseback, when running on uneven roads, on swampy ground, muddy rice fields, stony ground, or in a crowd of people. To hold the long sword in both hands is not the true Way, for if you carry a bow or spear or other arms in your left hand you have only one hand free for the long sword.

However, when it is difficult to cut an enemy down with one hand, you must use both hands. It is not difficult to wield a sword in one hand; the Way to learn this is to train with two long swords, one in each hand. It will seem difficult at first, but everything is difficult at first. Note that bows are difficult to draw, halberds are difficult to wield; as you become accustomed to the bow so your pull will become stronger. When you become used to wielding the long sword, you will gain the power of the Way and wield the sword well.

As I will explain in the second book, the Water Book, there is no fast way of wielding the long sword. The long sword should be wielded broadly, and the companion sword closely. This is the first thing to learn.

According to the Ichi School, you can win with a long or with a short weapon. The Way of the Ichi School is the spirit of winning, whatever the weapon and whatever its size.

It is better to use two swords rather than one when you are fighting a crowd and especially if you want to take a prisoner. These things are difficult to explain in detail, but when you attain the Way of strategy there will not be anything you cannot see; from one thing, you will know ten thousand things. You must study hard.

The Benefit of the Two Characters reading "Strategy"

Masters of the long sword are called strategists. As for the other military arts, those who master the bow are called archers, those who master the spear are called spearmen, those who master the gun are called marksmen, and those who master the halberd are called halberdiers. But we do not call masters of the Way of the long sword "longswordsmen", or "companionswordsmen".

Bows, guns, spears and halberds are all warriors' equipment and they are certainly part of strategy. However, to master the virtue of the long sword is to govern the world and oneself; thus the long sword is the basis of strategy. The principle is "strategy by means of the long sword". If one attains the virtue of the long sword, one man can beat ten men. As one man can beat ten, so a hundred men can beat a thousand, and a thousand men can beat ten thousand. In my strategy, one man is the same as ten thousand, so this strategy is the complete warrior's craft.

The Way of the warrior does not include other Ways, such as Confucianism, Buddhism, certain traditions, artistic accomplishments and sword dancing. But even though these are not part of the Way, if you know the Way broadly you will see it in everything. Men must polish their particular Way.

The Benefit of Weapons in Strategy

There is a time and a place for use of weapons. The best use of the companion sword is in a confined space, or when you are engaged closely with an opponent. The long sword can be used effectively in all situations. The halberd is inferior to the spear on the battlefield. With the spear you can take the initiative; the halberd is defensive. In the hands of one of two men of equal ability, the spear gives a little extra strength. Spear and halberd both have their uses, but neither is very beneficial in confined spaces.

They cannot be used for taking a prisoner. They are essentially weapons for the field.

If you learn "indoor" techniques, you will think narrowly and forget the true Way. Then you will have difficulty in actual encounters.

The bow is tactically strong at the commencement of battle, especially battles on a moor, as it is possible to shoot quickly from among the spearmen. However, it is unsatisfactory in sieges, or when the enemy is more than forty yards away. For this reason there are now few traditional schools of archery and there is little use nowadays for this kind of skill.

From inside fortifications, the gun has no equal among weapons. It is the supreme weapon on the field before the ranks clash, but once swords are crossed the gun becomes useless.

One of the virtues of the bow is that you can see the arrows in flight and correct your aim accordingly, whereas gunshot cannot be seen. You must appreciate the importance of this difference.

Weapons should be enduring and without defects. Swords and companion swords should cut strongly. Spears and halberds must stand up to heavy use. Bows and guns must be sturdy. Weapons should be hardy rather than decorative.

You should not have a favorite weapon, nor likes and dislikes. To become over-familiar with one weapon is as much a fault as not knowing it sufficiently well. You should not copy others, but use those weapons you can handle properly. These are things you must know completely.

Timing in strategy

There is timing in everything. Timing in strategy cannot be mastered without a great deal of practice.

Just as timing is important in dancing and pipe or string music - as they are in rhythm only if timing is good - timing and rhythm are also involved in the military arts, shooting bows and guns, and riding horses. In fact, all skills and abilities involve timing, and there is also timing in the Void.

There is timing in the whole life of the warrior, in his thriving and declining, in his harmony and discord. Similarly, there is timing in the Way of the merchant, in the rise and fall of capital. All things entail rising and falling timing. You must be able to discern this.

In strategy there are various timing considerations. To begin you must know the applicable timing and the inapplicable timing, the fast and slow timings, and find the relevant timing from among large and small things. Studying timing is an essential thing in strategy. It is especially important to know the background timing, otherwise your strategy will become uncertain.

You win in battles with the timing of cunning by knowing the enemies' timing, and using a timing which the enemy does not expect. All the five books are chiefly concerned with timing. You must train sufficiently to appreciate all this.

If you practice day and night in the above Ichi School strategy, your spirit will naturally broaden. This Way of strategy is recorded for the first time in the five books of Ground, Water, Fire, Tradition (Wind), and Void.

For men who want to learn my strategy, this is the Way:

- Do not think dishonestly.
- The Way is in training.
- Become acquainted with every art.
- Know the Ways of all professions.
- Distinguish between gain and loss in worldly matters.
- Develop intuitive judgment and understanding for everything.
- Perceive those things that cannot be seen.
- Pay attention even to trifles.
- Do nothing useless

It is important to start by setting these broad principles in your heart. You must train in the Way of strategy. If you do not look at things on a large scale, it will be difficult for you to master strategy; however if you learn and attain this strategy, you will never lose even to twenty or thirty enemies.

More than anything, you must set your heart on strategy and earnestly stick to the Way. By training you will be able to freely control your own body, conquer men with your body, and with sufficient training you will be able to beat men in fights, be able to win with your eye, and beat ten men with your spirit. When you have reached this point, will it not mean that you are invincible?

Further, in large scale strategy the superior man will manage many subordinates dexterously, bear himself correctly, govern the country and foster the people, thus preserving the ruler's discipline. Hence following the Way of strategy involves the spirit not being defeated, helping oneself and gaining honor.

The second year of Shoho (1645), the fifth month, the twelfth day.

The Ground Book

The Water Book

The spirit of the Ni Ten Ichi School of strategy is based on water, and this Water Book explains methods of victory in the long-sword form of the Ichi School. While language is inadequate to explain the Way in detail, it can be grasped intuitively. Think about each word as you study this book. If you interpret the meaning loosely you will mistake the Way.

While principles of strategy are written here in terms of single combat, you must think broadly so that you attain an understanding for ten-thousand-a-side battles. Strategy is different from other things in that if you mistake the Way even a little, you will become bewildered and fall into bad ways.

You will not reach the Way of strategy by merely reading this book. This book is meant to be studied, absorbed, memorized and imitated, so that you may truly grasp its principles from within your heart and absorb them into your body.

Spiritual Bearing in Strategy

In strategy your spiritual bearing must not be any different from normal. Both in fighting and in everyday life you should be determined though calm. Meet situations without tenseness yet not recklessly, your spirit settled yet unbiased. Even when your spirit is calm do not let your body relax, and when your body is relaxed do not let your spirit slacken. Do not let your spirit be influenced by your body, nor your body be influenced by your spirit. Be neither insufficiently spirited nor over spirited. An elevated spirit is weak and a low spirit is weak. Do not let the enemy see your spirit.

Small people must be completely familiar with the spirit of large people, and large people must be familiar with the spirit of small people. Whatever your size, do not be misled by the reactions of your own body. With your spirit open and unrestricted, look at things from a high point of view. Cultivate and polish your wisdom: learn public justice, distinguish between good and evil, and study the Ways of different arts one by one. When you are not deceived by men you will have realized the wisdom of strategy.

The wisdom of strategy is different from other things. You should ceaselessly research the principles of strategy so that you can develop a steady spirit.

Stance in Strategy

Adopt a stance with the head erect, neither hanging down, nor looking up, nor twisted. Your forehead and the space between your eyes should not be wrinkled. Do not roll your eyes nor allow them to blink, rather slightly narrow them. With your features composed, keep the line of your nose straight with a feeling of slightly flaring your nostrils. Hold the line of the rear of the neck straight; instill vigor into your hairline and from the shoulders down through your entire body. Lower both shoulders and, without the buttocks jutting out, put strength into your legs from the knees to the tops of your toes. Brace your abdomen so that you do not bend at the hips. Wedge your companion sword in your belt against your abdomen, so that your belt is not slack - this is called "wedging in".

In all forms of strategy, it is necessary to maintain the combat stance in everyday life and to make your everyday stance your combat stance. You must grasp this well.

The Gaze in Strategy

The gaze should be large and broad. This is the twofold gaze - "Perception and Sight". Perception is strong and sight weak.

In strategy it is important to see distant things as if they were close and to take a distanced view of close things. It is important to know the enemy's sword and not to be distracted by insignificant movements of his sword. You must study this. The gaze is the same for single combat and for large-scale combat.

It is necessary in strategy to be able to look to both sides without moving your eyeballs. You cannot master this ability quickly. Learn what is written here: use this gaze in everyday life and never vary from it.

Holding the Long Sword

Grip the long sword with a floating feeling in your thumb and forefinger, with the middle finger neither tight nor slack, and with the last two fingers tight.

When you take up a sword, you must feel intent on cutting the enemy. As you cut an enemy you must not change your grip, and your hands must not "cower". When you dash the enemy's sword aside, or ward it off, or force it down, you must slightly change the feeling in your thumb and forefinger. Above all, you must be intent on cutting the enemy in the way you grip the sword. The grip during combat and during sword-testing is the same.

Generally, I dislike fixedness in both long swords and hands. Fixedness means a dead hand. Pliability is a living hand. You must bear this in mind.

Footwork

With the tips of your toes somewhat floating, tread firmly with your heels. Whether you move fast or slow, with large or small steps, your feet must always move as in normal walking. I dislike the three walking methods known as "jumping-foot", "floating-foot" and "fixed-steps".

So-called "Yin-Yang foot" is important to the Way. Yin-Yang foot means moving both feet; it means moving your feet left-right and right-left when cutting, withdrawing, or warding off a cut. You should not move one foot preferentially.

The Five Attitudes

There are five dimensions of attitude, and there are no attitudes but these five. The five attitudes are: Upper, Middle, Lower, Right Side, and Left Side. The one purpose of all attitudes is to cut the enemy. Whatever attitude you are in, do not be conscious of making the attitude; think only of cutting.

Your attitude should be large or small according to the situation. Upper, Lower and Middle attitudes are decisive. Left Side and Right Side attitudes are fluid. Left and Right attitudes should be used if there is an obstruction overhead or to one side. The decision to use Left or Right depends on the place.

The Middle attitude is the heart of the attitudes, the essence of the Way. To understand attitude you must thoroughly understand the Middle attitude, for if we look at strategy on a broad scale, the Middle attitude is the seat of the commander, with the other four attitudes following the commander. You must comprehend this.

The Way of the Long Sword

To know the Way of the long sword means we can wield with two fingers the sword that we usually carry. If we know the path of the sword well, we can wield it easily.

To wield the long sword well you must wield it calmly. If you try to wield the long sword quickly, like a folding fan or a short sword, you will mistake the Way and you will err by using "short sword chopping". You cannot cut a man with a long sword using this method.

When you have cut downwards with the long sword, lift it straight upwards; when you cut sideways, return the sword along a sideways path. Return the sword in a reasonable way, always stretching the elbows broadly. Wield the

37

sword strongly. This is the Way of the long sword.

If you learn to use the five approaches of my strategy, you will be able to wield a sword well. You must train constantly.

The Five Approaches

- The first approach is the Middle attitude. Confront the enemy with the point of your sword against his face. When he attacks, dash his sword to the right and "ride" it. Or, when the enemy attacks, deflect the point of his sword by hitting downwards, keep your long sword where it is, and as the enemy renews the attack, cut his arms from below. This is the first method.

The five approaches are similar in purpose. You must train repeatedly using a long sword in order to learn them. When you master my Way of the long sword, you will be able to control any attack the enemy makes. I assure you, there are no attitudes other than the five attitudes of the long sword of NiTo.

- In the second approach with the long sword, use the Upper attitude and cut the enemy just as he attacks. If the enemy evades the cut, keep your sword where it is and, scooping from below, cut him as he renews the attack. It is possible to repeat the cut from here.

In this method there are various changes in timing and spirit. You will be able to understand this by training in the Ichi School. You will always win with the five long sword methods. You must train repeatedly.

- In the third approach, adopt the Lower attitude, anticipating scooping up. When the enemy attacks, hit his hands from below. As you do so, he may try to hit your sword down. If this is the case, cut his upper arm(s) horizontally with a feeling of "crossing". This means that from the Lower attitudes you hit the enemy at the instant that he attacks.

You will encounter this method often, both as a beginner and in later strategy. You must train holding a long sword.

- In this fourth approach, adopt the Left Side attitude. As the enemy attacks, hit his hands from below. If as you hit his hands he attempts to dash down your sword, parry the path of his long sword with the feeling of hitting his hands and cut across from above your shoulder.

This is the Way of the long sword. Through this method you win by parrying the line of the enemy's attack. You must study this.

- In the fifth approach, the sword is in the Right Side attitude. In accordance with the enemy's attack, cross your sword from below at the side to the Upper attitude. Then cut straight from above.

This method is essential for knowing the Way of the long sword well. If you can use this method, you can freely wield a heavy long sword.

I cannot describe in detail how to use these five approaches. You must become well acquainted with my "in harmony with the long sword" Way, learn large-scale timing, understand the enemy's long sword, and become accustomed to the five approaches. You will always win by using these five methods, with various timing considerations discerning the enemy's spirit. You must reflect upon all this carefully.

The "Attitude No-Attitude" Teaching

"Attitude No-Attitude" means that there is no need for what are known as long

sword attitudes. Even so, attitudes do exist as the five ways of holding the long sword. However you hold the sword, it must be in such a way that it is easy to cut the enemy well, in accordance with the situation, the place, and your relation to the enemy. From the Upper attitude, as your spirit lessens you can adopt the Middle attitude, and from the Middle attitude you can raise the sword a little in your technique and adopt the Upper attitude. From the Lower attitude you can raise the sword a little and adopt the Middle attitudes as the occasion demands. According to the situation, if you turn your sword from either the Left Side or Right Side attitude towards the center, the Middle or the Lower attitude results.

This principle is known as: "Existing Attitude - Non-existing Attitude".

The most important thing when you take a sword in your hands is your intention to cut the enemy, whatever the means. Whenever you parry, hit, spring, strike or touch the enemy's cutting sword, you must cut the enemy in the same movement. This is essential. If you think only of hitting, springing, striking or touching the enemy, you will not be able actually to cut him. More than anything, you must be thinking of carrying your movement through to cutting him. To achieve this you must research it well.

Attitude in strategy on a larger scale is called "Battle Array" and is intended for winning battles. Do not use a fixed formation. Study this well.

To Hit the Enemy "In One Timing"

When you have drawn close to the enemy, hit him as quickly and directly as possible, without moving your body or settling your spirit, while you see that he is still undecided. This timing of hitting before the enemy decides to withdraw, break or hit, is called "In One Timing".

It takes training to achieve this timing and to be able to hit in the timing of an instant.

The "Abdomen Timing of Two"

When you attack and the enemy quickly retreats, as you see him tense you must feint a cut. Then, as he relaxes, follow up and hit him. This is the "Abdomen Timing of Two". It is very difficult to attain this merely by reading this book, but you will soon understand with a little instruction.

No Design, No Conception

In this method, when the enemy attacks and you decide to attack, hit with your body, hit with your spirit, and hit from the Void with your hands, accelerating strongly. This is the "No Design, No Conception" cut.

This is the most important method of hitting. It is often used. You must train hard to understand it.

The Flowing Water Cut

The "Flowing Water Cut" is used when you are struggling blade to blade with the enemy. When he breaks and quickly withdraws trying to spring with his long sword, expand your body and spirit and cut him as slowly as possible with your long sword, following your body like stagnant water. You can cut with certainty if you learn this. You must discern the enemy's grade.

The Fire and Stones Cut

The Fires and Stones Cut means that when the enemy's long sword and your long sword clash together, you cut as strongly as possible without raising the sword even a bit. This means cutting quickly with the hands, body and legs - all three cutting strongly. If you train well enough you will be able to strike strongly.

The Red Leaves Cut

The Red Leaves Cut means knocking down the enemy's long sword. When the enemy is in a long sword attitude in front of you and intent on cutting, hitting and parrying, you strongly hit the enemy's sword with the Fire and Stones Cut, perhaps in the design of the "No Design, No Conception" Cut. The spirit should be getting control of his sword. If you then beat down the point of his sword with a sticky feeling, he will necessarily drop the sword. If you practice this cut it becomes easy to make the enemy drop his sword. You must train repetitively.

The Body in Place of the Long Sword

Also called: "the long sword in place of the body". Usually we move the body and the sword at the same time to cut the enemy. However, according to the enemy's cutting method, you can dash against him with your body first, and afterwards cut with the sword. If his body is immoveable, you can cut first with the long sword, but generally you hit first with the body and then cut with the long sword. You must examine this well and practice hitting.

Cut and Slash

To cut and slash are two different things. Cutting is decisive, with a resolute spirit. When you cut, your spirit is resolved. Slashing is nothing more than touching the enemy. Even if you slash strongly, and even if the enemy dies instantly, it is called slashing. If you first slash the enemy's hands or legs, you must then cut strongly. Slashing is in spirit the same as touching. When you understand this, they become indistinguishable. Learn this well.

Chinese Monkey's Body

The Chinese Monkey's Body is the spirit of not stretching out your arms. The spirit is to get in quickly with your whole body before the enemy attacks, without extending your arms in the least. When you come to within arm's reach it becomes easy to move your body in.

Glue and Lacquer Emulsion Body

The spirit of "Glue and Lacquer Emulsion Body" is to stick to the enemy and not separate from him. People tend to advance their head and legs quickly, but their body lags behind. Instead, when you approach the enemy, stick firmly with your head, body and legs. You should stick firmly so that there is not the slightest gap between the enemy's body and your body.

To Strive for Height

When you close with the enemy, strive with him for superior height without cringing. Stretch your legs, stretch your hips, and stretch your neck face to face with him. When you think you have won, and you are the higher, thrust in strongly. You must learn to execute this.

To Apply Stickiness

When both you and the enemy attack with the long sword, you should go in with a sticky feeling and fix your long sword against the enemy's as you receive his cut. The spirit of stickiness is not hitting very strongly, but hitting so that the long swords do not separate easily. It is best to approach as calmly as possible when hitting the enemy's long sword with stickiness. The difference between "Stickiness" and "Entanglement" is that stickiness is firm and entanglement is weak. It is important to understand this.

The Body Strike

The Body Strike means to approach the enemy through a gap in his guard. The spirit is to strike him with your body. Turn your face slightly aside and strike the enemy's breast with your left shoulder thrust out. Approach with a spirit of bouncing the enemy away, striking as strongly as possible in time with your breathing. If you succeed in this method of closing with the enemy, you will be able to knock him ten or twenty feet away. It is possible to strike the enemy until he is dead. Train vigorously.

Three Ways to Parry His Attack

There are three methods to parry a cut:

1) When the enemy makes an attack, dash his long sword to your right, as if thrusting at his eyes.

2) Parry by thrusting the enemy's long sword towards his right eye with the feeling of snipping his neck.

49

3) When you have a short "long sword", without worrying about parrying the enemy's long sword, close with him quickly by thrusting at his face with your left hand.

These are the three ways of parrying. You must bear in mind that you can always clench your left hand and thrust at the enemy's face with your fist. For this it is necessary to train well.

To Stab at the Face

When your spirit is intent on stabbing at the enemy's face, follow the line of the blades with the point of your long sword. If you are intent on stabbing at his face, his body will become disposable, presenting opportunities to win quickly. You must pursue the value of this technique through training.

To Stab at the Heart

The spirit of this principle is often useful when we become tired or for some reason our long sword will not cut. In fighting, if there are obstructions above or to the sides, and whenever it is difficult to cut, stabbing at the heart means to thrust at the enemy. You must stab the enemy's breast without letting the point of your long sword waver, showing the enemy the ridge of the blade square-on, and with the spirit of deflecting his long sword. You must be familiar with the application of this method.

To Scold "Tut-TUT!"

To "scold" means that when the enemy tries to counter-cut as you attack, you counter-cut again from below as if thrusting at him, trying to hold him down. With very quick timing you cut, scolding the enemy. Thrust up, "Tut!" and cut "TUT!" This timing is encountered time and time again in exchanges of blows. The way to scold "Tut-TUT" is to time the cut simultaneously with raising your long sword as if to thrust the enemy. This skill is acquired through repetitive practice.

The Smacking Parry

When you clash swords with the enemy, meet his attacking cut on your long sword with a tee-dum, tee-dum rhythm, smacking his sword and cutting him. The spirit of the smacking parry is not parrying, or smacking strongly, but smacking the enemy's long sword in accordance with his attacking cut, primarily intent on quickly cutting him. If you understand the timing of smacking, however hard your long swords clash, your sword point will not be knocked back even a little. You must study and train keenly in order to achieve this.

There are Many Enemies

"There are Many Enemies" applies when you are one fighting against many. Draw both sword and companion sword and assume a wide-stretched left and right attitude. The spirit is to chase the enemies from side to side, even though they come from all four directions. Observe their attacking order, and go to meet first those who attack first. Sweep your eyes around broadly, carefully examining the attacking order, and cut left and right alternately with your swords. Do not wait! Always quickly re-assume your attitudes to both sides, cutting the enemies down as they advance and crushing them in the direction from which they attack. Most importantly, aim to drive the enemy together, as if tying a line of fishes, and when they piled close together, cut them down strongly without giving them room to move.

One Cut

You can win with certainty with the spirit of "one cut", however it is difficult to attain this if you do not learn strategy well. If you train well in the Way, strategy will come from your heart and you will be able to win at will. You must train devotedly.

Direct Communication

The spirit of "Direct Communication" is how the true Way of the NiTo Ichi School is received and handed down. Strategy with the long sword cannot be clearly explained in writing, but through diligent practice you will understand how to win.

Oral tradition: "The true Way of strategy is revealed in the long sword."

Oral tradition: "Teach your body strategy."

Recorded in the above book is an outline of Ichi School sword fighting.

In summary, to learn how to win with the long sword in strategy, first learn the five approaches and the five attitudes, and absorb the Way of the long sword naturally in your body. You must understand spirit and timing, handle the long sword naturally, and move body and legs in harmony with your spirit. Whether beating one man or more, you will then appreciate the value of strategy.

Study the contents of this book taking one item at a time, and through fighting with enemies you will gradually come to know the principle of the Way.

Deliberately, with a patient spirit, absorb the virtue of the Way, occasionally raising your hand in combat. Maintain this spirit whenever you cross swords with an enemy.

Step by step walk the thousand-mile road.

Study strategy over the years and achieve the spirit of the warrior. Today is your victory over yourself of yesterday; tomorrow is your victory over lesser men.

In order to beat more skillful men, train intensely with the guidance of this book. Even if you kill an enemy, if it is not based on what you have learned it is not the true Way.

If you attain this Way of victory, you will be able to beat several tens of men. What remains is sword-fighting ability, which you can attain in battles and duels.

The Second Year of Shoho, the twelfth day of the fifth month (1645).

The Water Book

The Fire Book

I describe fighting as fire in this Fire Book of the NiTo Ichi School of strategy.

My Way of strategy is the sure method wherein "one man can beat ten; a thousand men can beat ten thousand". Of course, you cannot assemble a thousand or ten thousand men for everyday training. But you can become a master of strategy by training alone with a sword so that you can understand the enemy's strategies, his strengths and resources, and come to appreciate how to apply strategy to beat ten thousand enemies to win.

Most people think narrowly about the benefit of strategy. By using only their fingertips, they only know the benefit of three of the five inches of the wrist. They let a contest be decided merely by the span of their forearms, for they specialize in the small matter of dexterity, learning such trifles as hand and leg movements with the bamboo practice sword.

In my strategy, the training for killing enemies is by way of many contests, fighting for survival, discovering the meaning of life and death, learning the Way of the sword, judging the strength of attacks and understanding the Way of the "edge and ridge" of the sword. You cannot profit from small techniques particularly when full armor is worn.

Any man who wants to master the essence of my strategy must study diligently, training morning and evening. Thus can he polish his skill, become free from self, and realize extraordinary ability. He will come to possess miraculous power.

This is the practical result of strategy.

Depending on the Place

Examine your environment.

Take up an attitude with the sun behind you. If the situation does not allow this, you must try to keep the sun on your right side; or, if in buildings, stand with the entrance behind you or to your right. Make sure that your rear is unobstructed, and that there is free space on your left, your right side being occupied with your sword attitude. At night, if the enemy can be seen, keep the fire behind you and the entrance to your right, and otherwise take up your attitude as above. You must look down on the enemy, and take up your attitude on a slightly higher plane.

During a fight, always endeavor to chase the enemy around to your left side. Chase him towards awkward places - bad footholds, obstacles at the side, and so on - trying to keep him with his back to awkward places. When the enemy gets into an inconvenient position, do not let him look around, but conscientiously chase him around and pin him down. In houses, chase the enemy into the thresholds, lintels, doors, verandas, pillars, and so on, again not letting him see his situation. Use the virtues of each place to establish predominant positions from which to fight. You must research and train diligently in this.

The Three Methods to Forestall the Enemy

The first method is to forestall him by attacking. This is called Ken No Sen (to set him up).

Another method is to forestall him as he attacks. This is called *Tai No Sen* (to wait for the initiative).

The third method is when you and the enemy attack together. This is called *Tai Tai No Sen* (to accompany him and forestall him).

There are no methods of taking the lead other than these three. Since you can win quickly by taking the lead, this is one of the most important elements in strategy. There are several things involved in taking the lead. You must make the best of the situation, see through the enemy's spirit so that you grasp his strategy, and defeat him. It is impossible to fully explain this in writing.

The First - Ken No Sen

When you decide to attack, stay calm and dash in quickly, forestalling the enemy. Or, you can advance seemingly strongly but with a reserved spirit, forestalling him with the reserve.

Alternately, advance with as strong a spirit as possible, and when you reach the enemy move with your feet a little quicker than normal, unsettling him and overwhelming him sharply.

Or, with your spirit calm, attack with a feeling of constantly crushing the enemy, from first to last. The spirit is to win in the depths of the enemy.

These are all *Ken No Sen*.

The Second - Tai No Sen

When the enemy attacks, remain undisturbed but feign weakness. As the enemy approaches you, move away suddenly as if indicating that you intend to jump aside; then dash in attacking strongly as soon as you see the enemy relax. This is one way.

Or, as the enemy attacks, attack more strongly, taking advantage of the resulting disorder in his timing to win.

This is the *Tai No Sen* principle.

The Third - Tai Tai No Sen

When the enemy makes a quick attack, you must attack strongly and calmly, aim for his weak point as he draws near, and strongly defeat him.

Or, if the enemy attacks calmly, you must observe his movement and, with your body rather floating, join in with his movements as he draws near. Move quickly and cut him strongly.

This is *Tai Tai No Sen*

These things cannot be clearly explained in words. In these three ways of forestalling, you must judge each situation independently. In strategy, you have effectively won when you forestall the enemy, so you must study what is written here and train well to attain this.

To Hold Down a Pillow

In contests of strategy, you always want to lead the enemy about rather than be led about by the enemy. Obviously, the enemy will be endeavoring to do the same thing, but he cannot forestall you if you do not allow him to come out.

In strategy, you must stop the enemy as he attempts to cut; you must push down his thrust, and throw off his hold when he tries to grapple. This is the meaning of "to hold down a pillow"; it means not allowing the enemy's head to rise. When you have grasped this principle, you will see in advance whatever the enemy tries to bring about in the fight and suppress it. The spirit is to check his attack as soon as it begins.

The important thing in strategy is to suppress the enemy's useful actions but allow his useless actions. However, doing this alone is defensive. First, you must act according to the Way, suppress the enemy's techniques, foiling his plans, and thence command him directly. When you can do this you will be a master of strategy. You must train well and research "holding down a pillow".

Crossing at a Ford

"Crossing at a ford" means, for example, crossing the sea at a strait, knowing the route, knowing the soundness of your ship and the favor of the day. It means setting sail when conditions are good, and there is perhaps a favorable wind, or a tailwind. This spirit, if you attain it, applies to everyday life. You must always think of crossing at a ford.

In strategy also it is important to "cross at a ford". Discern the enemy's capability and, knowing your own strong points, "cross the ford" at the most advantageous place, as a good captain crosses a sea route. If you succeed in crossing at the best place, you may take your ease. To cross at a ford means to attack the enemy's weak point and to put yourself in an advantageous position. This is how to win in large-scale strategy. The spirit of crossing at a ford is necessary in both large- and small-scale strategy. You must examine this well.

To Know the Times

"To know the times" means to know the enemy's disposition in battle. Is it flourishing or waning? By observing the spirit of the enemy's men, you can discover the enemy's disposition and move your men into position accordingly, thereby fighting from a position of advantage.

In a duel, forestall the enemy and attack when you have recognized his school of strategy, perceived his quality, and his strong and weak points. If your ability to "know the times" is high, you will be able to attack in an unsuspecting manner, knowing his metre and modulation and the appropriate timing.

When you are thoroughly conversant with strategy, you will recognize the enemy's intentions and thus have many opportunities to win. You must sufficiently study this.

To Tread Down the Sword

"To tread down the sword" is a principle often used in strategy. In large-scale strategy, when the enemy first attacks by discharging bows and guns, it is difficult to attack if we are busy loading powder into our guns or notching our arrows. The spirit is to attack quickly while the enemy is still shooting with bows or guns. The spirit is to win by "treading down" as we receive the enemy's attack.

In single combat, we cannot get a decisive victory by cutting, with a "tee-dum tee-dum" feeling, in the wake of the enemy's attacking long sword. We must defeat him at the start of his attack, in the spirit of treading him down with the feet, so that he cannot rise again to the attack.

"Treading" does not simply mean treading with the feet. Tread with the body, tread with the spirit, and, of course, tread and cut with the long sword. You must achieve the spirit of not allowing the enemy to attack a second time. This is the spirit of forestalling in every sense. Once at the enemy, you should not aspire to merely strike him, but to cling after the attack. You must absorb this deeply.

To Know "Collapse"

Everything can collapse. Houses, bodies, and enemies all collapse when their rhythm becomes deranged. In large-scale strategy, when the enemy starts to collapse, you must pursue him without letting the opportunity pass by. If you fail to take advantage of your enemies' collapse, they may recover.

In single combat, the enemy sometimes loses timing and collapses. If you let this chance go by, he may recover and not be so negligent thereafter. Fix your eye on the enemy's collapse and chase him, attacking so that you do not let him recover. You must do this. The chasing attack is with a strong spirit. You must utterly cut the enemy down so that he does not recover his position. You must understand utterly how to cut down the enemy.

To Become the Enemy

"To become the enemy" means to think yourself into the enemy's position. In large-scale strategy, people are always under the impression that the enemy is strong, and so tend to become cautious. But if you have good soldiers, and if you understand the principles of strategy, and if you know how to beat the enemy, there is nothing to worry about.

In single combat also you must put yourself in the enemy's position. If you think, "Here is a master of the Way, who knows the principles of strategy" then you will surely lose. You must consider this deeply.

To Release Four Hands

"To Release Four Hands" is used when you and the enemy are contending with the same spirit, and the issue cannot be decided. Abandon this spirit and win through an alternative resource.

In large-scale strategy, when there is a "four hands" spirit, immediately throw away the current spirit and win with a technique the enemy does not expect.

Similarly, in single combat, when we think we have fallen into the "four hands" situation, we must defeat the enemy by changing our mind and applying a suitable technique according to his condition. You must be able to judge this.

To Move the Shade

"To move the shade" is used when you cannot see the enemy's spirit. In large-scale strategy, if you cannot see the enemy's position, indicate that you are about to attack strongly, so as to discover his resources. Once you observe his resources, it is then easy to defeat him with a different method.

In single combat, if the enemy takes up a rear or side attitude of the long sword so that you cannot see his intention, make a feint attack, and the enemy will show his long sword, thinking he sees your spirit. Benefiting from what you are shown, you can win with certainty. If you are negligent you will miss the timing. Research this well.

To Hold Down a Shadow

"Holding down a shadow" is used when you can see the enemy's attacking spirit. In large-scale strategy, when the enemy embarks on an attack, if you make a show of strongly suppressing his technique, he will change his mind. Then, altering your spirit, defeat him by forestalling him with a Void spirit.

Or, in single combat, hold down the enemy's strong intention with a suitable timing, and defeat him by forestalling him with this timing. Look well into this.

To Pass On

In large-scale strategy, when the enemy is agitated and shows an inclination to rush, do not be bothered in the least. Make a show of complete calmness, and the enemy will be taken in by this and will also relax. When you see that your spirit has been passed on, you can bring about the enemy's defeat by attacking strongly with a Void spirit.

In single combat, you can win by relaxing your body and spirit and then, taking advantage of the moment the enemy relaxes, attack strongly and quickly, forestalling him.

What is known as "getting someone drunk" is similar to this. You can also infect the enemy with a bored, careless, or weak spirit. Understand this and use it well.

To Cause Loss of Balance

Many things can cause a loss of balance - danger, hardship, and the element of surprise. In large-scale strategy it is important to cause loss of balance. Attack without warning where the enemy is not expecting it, and while his spirit is undecided, follow up your lead advantage and defeat him.

Or, in single combat, start by making a show of being slow, then suddenly attack strongly. Without allowing him time to breathe and to recover from the fluctuation of spirit, grasp the opportunity to win. Get the feel of this.

To Frighten

Fright often occurs, caused by the unexpected. In large-scale strategy you can frighten the enemy by shouting, making a small force seem large, or by threatening them from the flank without warning. These things all frighten. You can win by making best use of the enemy's frightened rhythm.

In single combat also, you must use the advantage of taking the enemy unawares by frightening him with your body, long sword, or voice to defeat him.

To Soak In

When you are struggling together with the enemy and you realize that you cannot advance, you should "soak in" and become one with the enemy. You can win by applying a suitable technique while you are mutually entangled.

In battles involving large numbers as well as in fights with small numbers, you can often win decisively with the advantage of knowing how to "soak" into the enemy, whereas, were you to draw apart, you would lose the chance to win. Study this well.

To Injure the Corners

It is difficult to move strong things by pushing directly, so you should "injure the corners". In large-scale strategy, it is beneficial to strike at the corners of the enemy's force, for if the corners are overthrown, the spirit of the whole body will be overthrown. To defeat the enemy you must follow up the attack when the corners have fallen.

In single combat, when you injure the "corners" of the enemy's body and weaken him, it is easy to collapse the enemy and to win. It is important to know how to do this, so you must practice keenly.

To Throw into Confusion

In large-scale strategy, our troops can confuse the enemy on the field. Observing the enemy's spirit, we can make him think, "Here? There? Like that? Like this? Slow? Fast?" Victory is certain when the enemy is caught up in a rhythm that confuses his spirit.

In single combat, we can confuse the enemy by attacking with varied techniques when the chance arises. Feint a thrust or cut, or make the enemy thing you are going close to him, and when he is confused you can easily win.

This is the essence of fighting, and you must research it deeply.

The Three Shouts

The voice is a thing of life. The voice shows energy. The three shouts are divided thus: before, during and after. Shout according to the situation.

In large-scale strategy, at the start of battle we shout as loudly as possible. During the fight, the voice is low-pitched, shouting out as we attack. After the contest, we shout in the wake of our victory. These are the three shouts.

In single combat, we make as if to cut and shout "Ei!" at the same time to disturb the enemy, then in the wake of our shout we cut with the long sword. We shout after we have cut down the enemy to announce victory. This is called "*sen go no koe*" (before and after voice). We do not shout simultaneously with flourishing the long sword. We shout during the fight to get into rhythm. Study this intensely.

To Mingle

'Mingling' is the spirit of advancing and becoming engaged with the enemy without retreating even one step. In battles, attack the enemy's strong points and when you see that they are beaten back, quickly separate and attack yet another strong point on the periphery of his force. The spirit of this is like a winding mountain path.

This is an important fighting method for one man against many. Strike down the enemies in one quarter, or drive them back, then grasp the timing and attack further strong points to right and left, as if on a winding mountain path, weighing the enemies' disposition. When you know the enemies' level, attack strongly with no trace of retreating spirit.

In single combat, too, use this spirit with the enemy's strong points.

To Crush

In large-scale strategy, when we see that the enemy has few men, or that he has many men but his spirit is weak and disordered, we knock the hat over his eyes, crushing him utterly. If we crush lightly, he may recover. You must learn the spirit of crushing as if with a hand-grip.

In single combat, if the enemy is less skillful, his rhythm disorganized, or if he has fallen into evasive or retreating attitudes, we must crush him immediately, without allowing him space to breathe. It is essential to crush him all at once. The essential thing is not to let him recover his position in the slightest.

The Mountain-Sea Change

The "mountain-sea" spirit means that it is poor strategy to repeat the same technique several times when fighting the enemy. If you must do something twice, do not try it a third time; for if you attack once and fail, there is little chance of succeeding if you use the same approach again. You must change your attacking method.

If the enemy thinks mountains, attack like the sea; and if he thinks of the sea, attack like mountains. You must research this deeply.

To Penetrate the Depths

The principle of "penetrating the depths" is to destroy the enemy's spirit. When we are fighting the enemy, even when it appears that we can win with the benefit of the Way, if his spirit is not extinguished he may be beaten superficially yet remain undefeated in spirit deep inside. Hence, we destroy the enemy's spirit in its depths, demoralizing him by quickly changing our spirit.

Penetrating the depths means penetrating with the long sword, penetrating with the body, and penetrating with the spirit. Once we have crushed the enemy in the depths, there is no need to remain spirited. But otherwise we must remain spirited. If the enemy remains spirited it is difficult to crush him. You must train in penetrating the depths for both large-scale and single combat strategy.

To Renew

"To renew" applies when we are fighting with the enemy and an entangled spirit arises where there is no possible resolution. In such a case we must abandon our efforts, think of the situation in a fresh spirit, and then win in the new rhythm. To renew when we are deadlocked with the enemy means that without changing our circumstance we change our spirit and win through a different technique.

It is necessary to consider how "to renew" also applies in large-scale strategy. Research this diligently.

Rat's Head, Ox's Neck

"Rat's head and ox's neck" means that, when we are fighting with the enemy and both he and we have become occupied with small points in an entangled spirit, we must always think of the Way of strategy as being both a rat's head and an ox's neck. Whenever we have become preoccupied with small details, we must suddenly change into a large spirit, interchanging large with small.

This is one of the essences of strategy. It is necessary that the warrior think in this spirit in everyday life. You must not depart from this spirit in large-scale strategy nor in single combat.

The Commander Knows the Troops

Using the wisdom of strategy, think of the enemy as your own troops. When you think in this way, you will be able to move the enemy at will and chase him around. Thus you become the general and the enemy becomes your troops. "The commander knows the troops" applies everywhere in fights in my Way of strategy. Master this.

To Let Go the Hilt

There are various kinds of spirit involved in letting go the hilt. There is the spirit of winning without a sword. There is also the spirit of holding the long sword but not winning. The various methods cannot be expressed in writing. You must train well.

The Body of a Rock

When you have mastered the Way of strategy, you can suddenly make your body like a rock, and then ten thousand things cannot touch or move you. This is the body of a rock.

All that is recorded above are my thoughts about Ichi School sword fencing, written down as the thoughts came to me. This is the first time I have written about my technique, and the order of things is a bit confused. It is difficult to express these concepts clearly.

This book is intended as a spiritual guide for the man who wishes to learn the Way. My heart has been inclined to the Way of strategy from my youth onwards. I have devoted myself to training my hand, tempering my body, and attaining the many spiritual attitudes of sword fencing.

If one observes men of other schools discussing theory and concentrating on techniques with the hands, although they seem skillful to watch, they have not the slightest true spirit. Of course, they think they are training the body and spirit, but it is an obstacle to the true Way, and its negative influence remains forever. Thus the true Way of strategy is degenerating and dying out.

The true Way of sword fencing entails the craft of defeating the enemy in a fight, and nothing other than this. If you attain and adhere to the wisdom of my strategy, you need never doubt that   you   will   win.
The second year of Shoho, the fifth month, the twelfth day (1645).

The Wind Book

In strategy, you must be familiar with the Ways of other schools, so I have written about various other traditions of strategy in this Wind Book.

Without knowledge of the Ways of other schools, it is difficult to understand the essence of my Ichi School. Looking at other schools, we find some that specialize in techniques of strength using extra-long swords; some study the Way of the short sword, known as *kodachi;* some teach dexterity in large numbers of sword techniques, teaching attitudes of the sword as the "surface" and the Way as the "interior".

However, in this book, in which I point out all the vices and virtues, and rights and wrongs, I will show that none of these are the true Way. My Ichi School is different. Other schools make success their means of livelihood, decoratively coloring articles in order to sell them. This is definitely not the Way of strategy.

Many of the world's strategists are concerned only with sword fencing, and limit their training to flourishing the long sword and carriage of the body. But is dexterity alone sufficient to win? This is not the essence of the Way.

I have recorded the unsatisfactory points of other schools one by one in this book. You must study these matters deeply to appreciate the benefit of my NiTo Ichi School.

Other Schools Using Extra-Long Swords

Some other schools have a liking for extra-long swords. From the point of view of my strategy these must be seen as weak schools, for they do not appreciate the principle of cutting the enemy by any means. Their preference is for the extra-long sword and, relying on the virtue of its length, they think of defeating the enemy from a distance.

In this world it is said, "One inch gives the hand advantage", but these are the idle words of one who does not know strategy. It shows the inferior strategy of a weak sprit that men should depend on the length of their sword, fighting from a distance without the benefit of strategy.

I expect there is a case for liking extra-long swords as part of a school's doctrine, but if we compare this with real life it is unreasonable. Surely we need not necessarily be defeated if we are using a short sword, and have no long sword?

It is difficult for these people to cut the enemy when at close quarters because of the length of the long sword. The large blade path makes the long sword an encumbrance, and they are at a disadvantage compared to the man armed with a short companion sword.

There is an old saying: "Great and small go together." I do not unconditionally dislike extra-long swords; what I dislike is the inclination towards the long sword. If we consider large-scale strategy, we can think of large forces in terms of long swords, and small forces as short swords. Cannot few men give battle against many? There are many instances of few men overcoming many.

If your heart is inclined to the long sword, your strategy is useless when called on to fight in a confined space, or if you are in a house armed only with your companion sword. Besides, some men have not the strength of others.

In my doctrine, I dislike preconceived, narrow spirit. You must study this well.

The Strong Long Sword Spirit in Other Schools

You should not speak of strong and weak long swords. If you are concerned with the strength of your sword, you will try to cut unreasonably strongly, and will not be able to cut at all. It is equally bad to try to cut strongly when testing the sword.

Whenever you cross swords with an enemy you must not think of cutting him either strongly or weakly; think only of cutting and killing him. Be intent solely on killing the enemy.

If you rely on strength, when you hit the enemy's sword you will inevitably hit too hard. If you do this, your own sword will be carried along as a result. Thus the saying, "The strongest hand wins", has no meaning.

In large-scale strategy, if you have a strong army and are relying on strength to win, but the enemy also has a strong army, the battle will be fierce. This is the same for both sides. Without the correct principle the fight cannot be won.

The spirit of my school is to win through the wisdom of strategy, paying no attention to trifles. Learn this well.

Use of the Shorter Long Sword in Other Schools

Using a shorter long sword is not the true Way to win.

In ancient times, tachi and katana meant long and short swords. Men of superior strength in the world can wield even a long sword lightly, so there is no case for their liking the short sword. They also make use of the length of spears and halberds. Some men use a shorter long sword with the intention of jumping in and stabbing the enemy at the unguarded moment when he flourishes his sword. This inclination is not the true Way.

To aim for the enemy's unguarded moment is completely defensive, and undesirable at close quarters with the enemy. Furthermore, you cannot use the method of jumping inside his defense with a short sword if there are many enemies. Some men think that if they go against many enemies with a shorter long sword they can unrestrictedly frisk around cutting in sweeps, but they have to parry cuts continuously, and eventually become entangled with the enemy. This is inconsistent with the true Way of strategy.

The sure Way to win is rather to chase the enemy around in a confusing manner, causing him to jump aside, with your body held strongly and straight. The same principle applies to large-scale strategy. The essence of strategy is to fall upon the enemy in large numbers and to bring about his speedy downfall.

Through their study of strategy, people of the world became accustomed to countering, evading and retreating as the normal thing. Becoming set in this habit, they are easily paraded around by the enemy. The Way of strategy is straight and true. You must chase the enemy around and make him obey your spirit.

Other Schools with many Methods of using the Long Sword

In order to gain the admiration of beginners, other schools teach that there are many methods of using the long sword. This is selling the Way. It is a vile spirit in strategy.

The reason for this is that to deliberate over many ways of cutting down a man is an error. To begin with, killing is not the Way of mankind. Killing is the same for people who are experienced fighters and for those who are not. It is the same for women or children, and there are not many different methods. We can speak of different tactics such as stabbing and mowing down, but only of these.

Anyway, cutting down the enemy is the Way of strategy, and there is no need for many refinements of it.

Even so, according to the place, your long sword may be obstructed above or to the sides, so you will need to hold your sword in such a manner that it can be used. There are five methods to win, in five directions. Methods apart from these five - hand twisting, body bending, jumping out, and so on, to cut the enemy - are not the true Way of strategy. In order to cut the enemy you must not make twisting or bending cuts. These are completely useless.

In my strategy, I bear my spirit and body straight, and cause the enemy to twist and bend. The necessary spirit is to win by attacking the enemy when his spirit is warped. You must understand this well.

Use of Attitudes of the Long Sword in Other Schools

Placing a great deal of importance on the attitudes of the long sword is a mistaken way of thinking. Attitudes are defensive techniques for situations in which you are not to be moved. That is, for garrisoning castles, battle array, and so on, showing the spirit of not being moved even by a strong assault. I dislike the defensive spirit known as "attitude".

In the Way of dueling, however, you must always be intent upon taking the lead and attacking. Attitude is the spirit of awaiting an attack. You must appreciate this.

In duels of strategy you must move the opponent's attitude: Attack where his spirit is lax, throw him into confusion, irritate and terrify him. Take advantage of the enemy's rhythm when he is unsettled and you can win.

I dislike the defensive spirit known as "attitude", therefore in my Way, there is something called "Attitude-No Attitude".

In large-scale strategy we deploy our troops for battle bearing in mind our strength, observing the enemy's numbers, and noting the details of the battlefield. This is at the start of the battle.

The spirit of attacking is completely different from the spirit of being attacked. Bearing an attack well, with a strong attitude, and parrying the enemy's attack well, is like making a wall of spears and halberds. When you attack the enemy, your spirit must go to the extent of pulling the stakes out of a wall and using them as spears and halberds. You must examine this well.

Fixing the Eyes in Other Schools

Some schools maintain that the eyes should be fixed on the enemy's long sword; some fix the eye on the hands, some on the face, some on the feet, and so on. If you fix the eyes on these places your spirit can become confused, and your strategy thwarted.

I will explain this in detail. Football players do not fix their eyes on the ball, but by knowing how to play well they perform well. When you become accustomed to something, you are not limited to the use of your eyes. People such as master musicians have the music score in front of their nose, but this does not mean that they fix their eyes on it specifically. Similarly, fighters flourish the sword in several ways when they have mastered the Way, but this does not mean that they make pointless movements of the sword. It means that they can perform naturally.

In the Way of strategy, once you have fought many times you will easily be able to appraise the speed and position of the enemy's sword, and having mastery of the Way you will see the weight of his spirit. In strategy, fixing the eyes means gazing at the man's heart.

In large-scale strategy the area to observe is the enemy's strength. "Perception" and "sight" are the two methods of seeing. Perception consists of concentrating strongly on the enemy's spirit, observing the condition of the battle field, fixing the gaze strongly, seeing the progress of the fight and the changes of advantage. This is the sure way to win.

In single combat you must not fix the eyes on details. As I said before, if you fix your eyes on details and neglect important things, your spirit will become bewildered, and victory will escape you. Research this principle well and train diligently.

Use of the Feet in Other Schools

There are various methods of using the feet: floating foot, jumping foot, springing foot, treading foot, crow's foot, and such nimble walking methods. From the point of view of my strategy, these are all unsatisfactory.

I dislike floating foot because the feet always tend to float during the fight. The Way must be trod firmly. Neither do I like jumping foot, because it encourages the habit of jumping, and a jumpy spirit. However much you jump, there is no real justification for it. Springing foot causes a springing spirit which is indecisive. Treading foot is a "waiting" method which I especially dislike.

Apart from these, there are various fast walking methods, such as crow's foot, and so on. However, sometimes you may encounter the enemy on marshland, swampy ground, river valleys, stony ground, or narrow roads, situations in which you cannot jump or move the feet quickly.

In my strategy, the footwork does not change. I always walk as I usually do in the street. You must never lose control of your feet. Move fast or slowly according to the enemy's rhythm, adjusting your body only as needed.

Carrying the feet is also important in large-scale strategy, for if you attack quickly and thoughtlessly without knowing the enemy's spirit, your rhythm will become deranged and you will not be able to win. Or, if you advance too slowly, you will not be able to take advantage of the enemy's disorder, the opportunity to win will escape, and you will not be able to finish the fight quickly. You must win by seizing upon the enemy's disorder and derangement, and by not according him even the slightest hope of recovery. Practice this well.

Speed in Other Schools

Speed is not part of the true Way of strategy. Whatever the Way, the master of strategy does not appear fast.

Some people can walk as fast as a hundred or a hundred and twenty miles in a day, but this does not mean that they run continuously from morning till night. Unpracticed runners may seem to have been running all day, but their performance is poor.

In the Way of dance, accomplished performers can sing while dancing, but when beginners try this they slow down and their spirit becomes busy. Very skillful people can manage a fast rhythm, but if you try to beat too quickly you will get out of time. Of course, slowness is also bad. Truly skilled people never get out of rhythm, are always deliberate, and never appear busy. From this example, the principle can be seen.

Speed is especially counterproductive in the Way of strategy. The reason for this is that depending on the place - marsh or swamp and so on - it may not be possible to move the body and legs together quickly. If you have a long sword in this situation you will be able to cut quickly even less, and if you try to cut quickly, as if using a fan or short sword, you will actually not cut at all. You must appreciate this.

In large-scale strategy, a fast, busy spirit is also undesirable. The spirit must be that of holding down a pillow, for then you will not be even a little off time.

When your opponent is hurrying recklessly, you must act contrarily and stay calm, without being influenced by the opponent. Train diligently to attain this spirit.

"Interior" and "Surface" in Other Schools

The artistic accomplishments usually claim surface meaning, and inner meaning (secret tradition) or "interior" and "gate", but in my Way of strategy, there is no "interior", nor "surface".

In combat there is no such thing as fighting on the surface, or cutting with the interior. When I teach my Way, I first train pupils in techniques that are easy for them to understand, and gradually endeavor to explain the deep principles, according to the pupil's progress. In any event, because the way to understanding is through experience, I do not speak of "interior" and "gate".

In this world, if you go into the mountains, and decide to go deeper and yet deeper, instead you will emerge at the gate. Whatever is the Way, it has an interior, and it is sometimes a good thing to point out the gate. In strategy, we cannot say what is concealed and what is revealed.

Perceiving the ability of my pupils, I teach the direct Way, remove the bad influence of other schools, and gradually introduce them to the true

Way of the warrior. The method of teaching my strategy is with a trustworthy spirit.

In the above sections, I have tried to record an outline of the strategy of other schools. I could continue by giving a specific accounting of these schools one by one, from the "gate" to the "interior", but I have intentionally not named the schools or their main points. The reason for this is that different branches of schools give different interpretations of the doctrines. In as much as men's opinions differ, so there must be differing ideas on the same matter. Thus no one man's conception is valid for any school.

I have shown the general tendencies of other schools on nine points. If we look at them from an honest viewpoint, we see that people tend to like long swords or short swords, and become concerned with strength in both large and small matters. You can see why I do not deal with the "gates" of other schools.

In my Ichi School of the long sword there is neither gate nor interior. There is no inner meaning in sword attitudes. You must simply keep your spirit true to realize the virtue of strategy.

Twelfth day of the fifth month, the second year of Shoho (1645).

The Book of the Void

The spirit of the void is where there is nothing. By knowing things that exist, you can know that which does not exist. That is the void. It is not part of man's general knowledge.

People in this world look at things mistakenly, thinking that what they do not understand must be the void. This is not the true void. It is bewilderment. Similarly, in the Way of strategy, there are warriors who think that whatever they cannot understand in their craft is the void. This is not the true void.

To attain the Way of strategy as a warrior you must train completely in other martial arts and not deviate for a moment from Way of the warrior. Practice day in and day out with a settled spirited. Polish the twofold spirit heart and mind, and sharpen the twofold gaze perception and sight. When your spirit is no longer foggy, when the clouds of bewilderment clear away, there is the true void.

Until you realize the true Way, whether it be Buddhism or common sense, you may think that things are correct and in order. However, if we look at things objectively, from the viewpoint of laws of the world, we see various doctrines departing from the true Way. Know well this spirit, with forthrightness as the foundation and the true spirit as the Way. Enact strategy broadly, correctly and openly.

You will then come to think of things in a wide sense and, taking the void as the Way, you will see the Way as void.

The void consists only of virtue, and no evil. Wisdom exists, principle exists, the Way exists; spirit is nothingness.

Twelfth day of the fifth month, second year of Shoho (1645)

CPSIA information can be obtained
at www.ICGtesting.com
Printed in the USA
BVHW031444061119
563063BV00002B/76/P